IMAGES
of Wales

MUMBLES

Valerie Owen and Marjorie Davies at a Girls' Friendly Society concert, *c.* 1949.

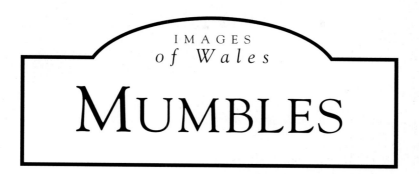

IMAGES
of Wales

MUMBLES

David Gwynn

TEMPUS

A nineteenth-century engraving of the *Velindra* off Mumbles Head.

First published 2003

Tempus Publishing Limited
The Mill, Brimscombe Port,
Stroud, Gloucestershire, GL5 2QG

British Library Cataloguing in Publication Data.
A catalogue record for this book is available from the British Library.

ISBN 0 7524 2858 6

Typesetting and origination by Tempus Publishing Limited
Printed in Great Britain by Midway Colour Print, Wiltshire

Contents

A coat of arms taken from a 1905 postcard. It is not possible to vouch for the provenance of this coat of arms.

Introduction

Mumbles today is a thriving suburb of the City and County of Swansea. Taking its name from the two little islets that form the western end of Swansea Bay, Mumbles now encompasses the villages of Oystermouth, Newton, West Cross and Norton as well as the bays at Langland, Rotherslade, Bracelet and part of Caswell.

Oystermouth has a long history, as there were Roman villas in the area prior to the end of Roman rule in about AD 410. The Normans arrived at the end of the eleventh century, erecting a wooden motte and bailey castle. Its stone-built successor, although now a ruin, stands on the same site, dominating the village.

By the eighteenth century, in addition to fishing, coal and iron ore were being mined in the nearby Clyne Valley, and limestone was being quarried at Norton and other sites. The famed Mumbles Marble is a particularly high-quality limestone that can be polished and used as a cheaper alternative to Italian marble. It was especially popular in Victorian times for fireplaces and ornate features in large homes.

Swansea in the eighteenth century was a genteel seaside resort and the birthplace of Beau Nash. Oystermouth was a distant fishing village. However, the Industrial Revolution was underway, and a development was about to occur that would change Mumbles quite dramatically. The coal and iron ore that was being mined in the Clyne Valley had to be transported to the docks at Swansea quickly and efficiently. To this end the Oystermouth Railway was launched in 1804, with horse-drawn wagons hauling the minerals to Swansea. The Oystermouth Railway was not the first mineral railway in Britain, but in 1807 there began a service which was to bring it world-wide renown – it began carrying passengers. A 'gentleman of Swansea' named Benjamin French was the instigator, and he should perhaps be much better known than he is, for he was the first person in the world to use a railway to carry fare-paying passengers on a regular service.

The Oystermouth Railway enjoyed a period of prosperity but by 1826 had fallen on hard times, effectively closing the following year and not reopening until 1860. Although still horse-drawn, the railway soon adopted the great motive power of the age, and in 1877 steam-hauled trains began running. This was the turning point, as the faster services brought Oystermouth within easy reach and it became a fashionable resort. In 1898, the line was extended to the newly-built Mumbles Pier. Tourists poured into Mumbles, and the postcard producers of the age made sure that there were plenty of cards to post home to friends and relatives. The early years of the twentieth century were the golden age of the picture postcard, and collecting postcards was a popular hobby. Local photographers such as M.A. Clare recorded just about everything that happened and gave us a legacy of invaluable material for study.

In 1929 the Mumbles Railway was electrified and the new electric cars could make the journey from Rutland Street to Mumbles Pier in just nineteen minutes. This made commuting a feasible proposition, and Mumbles began to grow as more and more people built houses in the area. The growth of the communities in Mumbles meant more shops, more hustle and bustle and of course, with the closing of the Mumbles Railway in 1960, more cars and buses.

In compiling this book I have included a great many postcards, as they are such an important resource when trying to show what an area looked like in the past. I have also been fortunate in being able to borrow interesting photographs that I hope every reader will enjoy. All too often old photographs and postcards are thrown out during house clearances or removal. That is very sad, as often they are the only record of what a place looked like in the past, and what people were doing as they went about their daily lives.

Mumbles has a fascinating history. I hope that these pictures will provide little windows on its past, bringing both enjoyment and understanding.

Acknowledgements

I would like to thank the following people who helped me in the compilation of this book: Peter Muxworthy; Diana Meyrick; Ken Reeves; Mrs G.E. Page; Mrs V.J. Peters; Malcolm Harrington; Mrs Alison Bastion, head teacher at Newton Primary School; Mrs N Martell, head teacher at Grange Primary School; Mr E.W. Wynne and Mrs M. Canning, head teacher and school clerk at Oystermouth Primary School; Peter Hixson, Hon. Secretary of Mumbles Rugby Football Club; Carol Powell; Tony Cottle; Pat Hill and the late Barbara John.

I would also like to thank my wife Alicia for her support and encouragement, and my children Caitlin, Rebecca and Steffan, all of whom helped in their own way.

David Gwynn 2003

One
Caswell Bay
to Bracelet Bay

Caswell Bay, *c.* 1900. The windmill on top of the hill was burnt down in 1930. Until 1918 the boundary between the Gower Rural District Council and the Oystermouth Urban District Council divided Caswell Bay. In that year, Oystermouth Urban District was absorbed into the County Borough of Swansea. In 1969 Swansea became a city and in 1974 it absorbed the Gower Rural District too.

Caswell Bay, *c.* 1905. The stone-built pumping station can be seen tucked under the cliff at the water's edge. The name Caswell is thought to derive from the Carswell stream, which runs down Caswell Valley and joins the sea at Caswell Bay. In turn, Carswell derives its name from the large amount of wild watercress once found along its banks.

Caswell Bay after the storm of 16 December 1910. As can be seen, the damage was extensive and the beach was covered with a large amount of debris.

Caswell Bay, *c*. 1930. In this view additional buildings can be seen next to the pumping station and on the foreshore. The frames of beach huts are also visible.

Caswell Hill, Mumbles, *c.* 1910. Another photograph by M.A. Clare, this time showing the road to Newton.

Entitled 'A peep at Caswell, Mumbles', this picture was taken by M.A. Clare of Mumbles from the hill leading to Bishopston.

Caswell Bay Hotel, *c.* 1920, seen from the beach. The Victorian villa that grew to become the hotel was built in 1850.

Caswell Bay, *c.* 1955. The growth in tourists to the area led to the provision of more services at Caswell, including a café, shops and more space for cars. Today Caswell remains one of the most popular of the Gower beaches.

Caswell Valley, *c.* 1910. The number of people who can be seen walking and picnicking in the valley shows how popular the area was with day trippers and holidaymakers in the early years of the twentieth century.

'Havergal', Caswell, *c.* 1910. This house was built by a John Tucker of Langland after 1874 and was originally called Park Villa. In October 1878 two sisters from Worcester, Maria and Frances Ridley Havergal came to lodge at the house. Frances Ridley Havergal was a well-known hymn writer and Christian poet, but she died at the house on 3 June 1879. Around 1913 the name of the house was changed to 'Havergal' and in 1937 a memorial plaque was fixed on the garden wall.

Caswell Valley, *c*. 1920. This view, taken looking up the valley, again shows crowds of people enjoying the fine weather. The house is Caswell Lodge, built by Sir John Dillwyn Llewellyn, who acquired the land in 1847. It was demolished to make way for the car park around 1960.

Summercliff camp, Caswell, *c*. 1930. The site of this temporary camp is now occupied by permanent chalets.

Beach shops at Langland, *c.* 1905. This postcard shows in detail the various goods on sale – perhaps not so different from today, with beach balls, buckets and spades, fishing nets and refreshments.

View of the cliffs between Caswell Bay and Langland Bay, showing the cliff path, around 1910.

Langland Bay, *c.* 1920. This postcard view actually shows more of Rotherslade than Langland, as it was taken from the sands at Langland. In the seventeenth century there was a farm in this area called Longeland, and it seems that the name Langland is a corruption of this.

Rotherslade, Langland, *c.* 1930. The now-demolished Osborne Hotel dominates this view, with Kifts Refreshment Rooms at the top of the beach.

Langland Bay Hotel, *c.* 1910. Photographed by M.A. Clare, this Victorian Gothic building dominated Langland.

Ticket to the ballroom at the Langland Bay Hotel. Unfortunately this example has not been dated, but it must be from before 1922 as the hotel closed in that year.

Langland Bay Convalescent Homes, Mumbles

In April 1922 the Club and Institute Union Ltd reopened the former Langland Bay Hotel as their fourth convalescent home. Postcard views of the building abound, this one dating from around 1925.

LANGLAND BAY HOME 25-7-22   80   M.H.CLARE MUMBLES

Taken on 25 July 1922 this picture probably shows the first group of residents, brought to Langland to recover by the sea from illness or injury.

A number of postcards exist showing interior views of the convalescent home. The Club and Institute Union themselves published a series of sepia postcards, but this is by the local photographer M.A. Clare and shows the smoking room.

This 1960 postcard shows a clear view of the convalescent home, but also shows the beach huts, both permanent and temporary, that range along the top of the beach at Langland.

Langland AFC, 1912/13 season.

Four young women pose outside one of
the beach huts in the summer of 1939.

SS *Tyne* aground at Langland, 19 April 1919. In heavy fog she collided with the *Fleur de Mer* which was cut in two. The *Tyne* was searching for the crew of the stricken ship when she herself went off course and ran aground. Ten days later she was refloated and towed to Swansea for repairs.

Tennis at Langland, 1964.

Henfaes, Rotherslade, *c.* 1930.

Henfaes, Rotherslade, *c.* 1950. As can be seen, the building had been altered in the intervening years to provide extra accommodation above the side porch.

23

Camptown, Limeslade, c. 1910. These camps were the precursors of the wooden chalets and bungalows that were built at Limeslade between the wars.

Limeslade Bay, c. 1915. Just above the bay two adjacent fields carry the name 'Limeslade' and it is from these that the bay seems to have acquired its name. The word 'slade' has several meanings, and is found in a number of Gower place names, most often associated with small, rocky bays. Limestone was quarried all along the south Gower coast, and was shipped out to Somerset, North Devon and Cornwall from the bays. Perhaps Limeslade was so named because it was a small bay from which limestone was shipped.

Limeslade Bay, *c.* 1932.

View of Langland from above Rotherslade, 1974. The beach huts and the tennis courts can be clearly seen.

Limeslade camps, *c.* 1930. A variety of buildings were erected in the fields at Limeslade.

Limeslade Bungalows, *c.* 1930.

Limeslade Bay, *c.* 1932.

Limeslade Bungalows, *c.* 1935.

Bracelet Bay and Mumbles Head, *c.* 1910. As the first bay reached after leaving Mumbles, Bracelet has always been a popular spot.

This photograph probably dates from the 1920s and is thought to have been taken at Limeslade. It shows a carnival float modelled on the tugboat *Swansea Castle*. The sail at the front of the boat carries some words, but it is not possible to read them all. It seems to exhort people to 'Assist the [Red Cross] by keeping fit. Eat more [fruit]'.

Mumbles Head and cliff, c. 1925. These are the cliffs and rocks between Limeslade and Bracelet Bay.

Limeslade Bungalows, c. 1930. This view shows some of the more solidly-built houses that overlook Limeslade.

At the same time as the Mumbles Pier was built, the road from Oystermouth and Southend was extended past the pier and around Mumbles Head to Bracelet Bay and Limeslade. This postcard from around 1905 shows the new road with Mumbles Head in the background. The road ends at Limeslade, where a sharp right-hand turn takes motorists into Plunch Lane. Originally the plan had been to continue the new road around the cliffs to Langland, but the Duke of Beaufort, as landowner, would not allow this to be done.

Motoring on the new road at Bracelet, c. 1905. It is thought that 'Bracelet' is a corruption of 'Broadslade', the original name of the bay having been Broadslade Bay.

Two

Mumbles Head
to Oystermouth

Mumbles from the air, c. 1964. A hundred years earlier, and this view would have shown a pattern of farms with neatly-hedged fields being the predominant aspect of the landscape. The decline of farming, as housing developments have spread, has led to a rise in the number of trees growing on the higher ground.

The Lighthouse, Mumbles, *c.* 1910.

Bob's Cave, on the outer island, Mumbles Head, *c.* 1905.

The Cutting, Mumbles, *c.* 1905. The Cutting was created when the new road was built around Mumbles Head to Bracelet Bay.

Mumbles Head, *c.* 1910, showing the two islets that give the area its name.

The natural arch, Mumbles Head, *c.* 1910.

Another view of the Cutting, *c.* 1905.

On the pier, Mumbles, *c.* 1910. The building of the pier in 1898 proved a draw for trippers and holidaymakers and put Mumbles firmly on the map as a seaside resort.

Mumbles Head from the pier, *c.* 1905.

Postcards of Mumbles Pier are very common, and a study of them will show the development of the pier over the years. Dating from 1905, this postcard shows the pleasure steamer *Brighton* calling at the pier.

This postcard, dating from 1910, shows the newly-built Mumbles Pier station building and other buildings at the entrance to the pier.

A lifeboat slip was added to the pier in 1916. From this postcard it is also possible to get a good impression of the amount of shipping that sailed through the Mumbles Roads on its way to the docks at Swansea.

Moving on to 1918, this postcard shows the Mumbles train at the station, but no building, and a glazed pavilion at the entrance to the pier. The station building was demolished during the First World War, and replaced with a smaller kiosk.

1922, and the lifeboat house has been built on the slip.

The old shoreline at Southend, *c.* 1900.

The *Marie Eugenie* of Bridgewater moored at high tide off Southend around 1910.

Another view of the shoreline at Southend, *c.* 1900.

The lighthouse had also changed dramatically by 1974, with many of the buildings removed.

By the 1950s the pier itself was largely unchanged, but a new café building and waiting area had been built at the end of the railway. The railway had been electrified in 1929. Various famous people have links with Mumbles: Sir Harry Secombe met his wife, Lady Myra, on Mumbles Pier in 1946;

Dylan Thomas was known to have frequented public houses in Mumbles and Catherine Zeta Jones has links with the area.

By 1974, the buildings on the pier had gone and an amusement arcade had opened near the pier entrance.

The Parade, Southend, *c.* 1905, showing the Parade Dining Rooms.

Parade Gardens, Southend, *c.* 1918.

Southend, *c.* 1920, showing the London Dining Room and the Mermaid Hotel.

The foreshore from Southend, *c.* 1960.

The seafront at Southend, *c.* 1905. The original Mumbles post office was probably opened at Southend as early as 1843. It remained here until 1906, when it moved to a site near Oystermouth Square. The Dunns post office was then closed and a sub-office opened at Southend, which lasted until 1959.

The Parade, Southend, *c.* 1908, showing the Shoulder of Mutton Dining Rooms.

A southerly view of The Parade, c. 1930.

The seafront at Southend, c. 1950.

The Prince's Fountain can be seen on the left of this picture. It was erected to mark the marriage on 10 March 1863 of Edward, Prince of Wales and Alexandra of Schleswig-Holstein-Sonderburg-Glucksburg, of the Danish royal family.

The Mermaid Hotel, c. 1924. This is an interesting postcard as the message on the reverse reads: 'The hotel we had decided to stay at has been turned into a Working Mens' Convalescent Home and we had to come back here.'

Seafront at Southend, 1977 – the boat in the foreground is the University College of Swansea Sailing Club rescue boat.

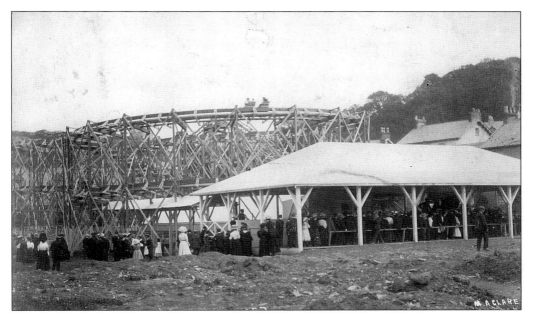

The Figure 8 Railway, Mumbles, *c.* 1902.

The Figure 8 Railway, Mumbles, *c.* 1912. The structure was later removed to Porthcawl.

The Dunns, Mumbles, *c.* 1880.

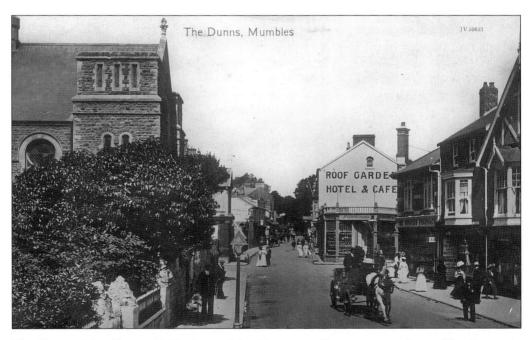

The Dunns, Mumbles, *c.* 1910. A new Mumbles post office was opened near The Dunns in 1906, opposite Claremont Villas. The Dunns post office, which had been operating since 1891, was closed, despite the objections raised by the sub-postmaster, W.H. Jones.

Oystermouth, c. 1880, with fishing boats hauled up on the beach and Portland Place in the right-hand foreground. Although damaged, the picture is a valuable record because of its early date.

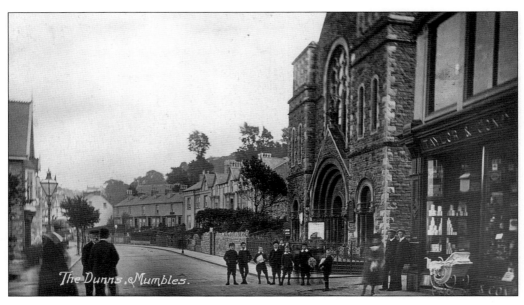

The Dunns, Mumbles, c. 1910. The houses in the middle distance have given way to a parade of shops and the present post office was built adjacent to the Methodist church in the 1950s.

Loading limestone at Oystermouth, *c.* 1900. Oystermouth is known as Ystum Llwynarth in Welsh, and may have derived from that Welsh name, which means 'bend by the enclosure'. However, as the name Oystermouth is recorded as early as 1284, it could be argued that the name was coined to reflect the oyster-fishing industry of the area.

Newton Road, *c.* 1955. Today this is the principal shopping street in Mumbles.

Oystermouth and Southend foreshore, photographed in 1977. A popular boating area, Mumbles boasts two yacht clubs – the Mumbles Yacht Club and the Bristol Channel Yacht Club.

Mumbles viewed from the quarry at Norton, around 1900. In the centre can be seen the shop of J. Eley, family butchers, and next to it the Oystermouth Coffee Tavern. A little further into the distance is seen the jetty used by local fishermen. The newly-built pier stands at the far end of the bay.

This 1930s view, also taken from the quarry, has Oystermouth Castle within shot and an increasingly developed Mumbles spreading along the bay.

Again taken from the quarry, this 1950 view shows an ivy-clad castle dominating the village below it.

Castleton and Oystermouth Castle, *c*. 1905. Shops now fill the area of Newton Road near the castle.

This 1950s view of Oystermouth shows the developments that took place in the post-war years at West Cross and Norton (in the background) and also around the castle.

Early postcards of Oystermouth Castle show an area of rural idyll. This postcard dates from around 1905.

The ivy seems to be out of control in this 1910 interior view of Oystermouth Castle.

Transfer of the castle into the care of the local authority meant that by 1974 the ancient walls were clear of ivy and other growth and the grounds were neat and well maintained.

Dated 1911, this postcard shows an event taking place at Underhill Park, Mumbles. There is no indication as to what the event is, but it could be a celebration of the Coronation of King George V and Queen Mary, which took place that year.

Oystermouth Castle and its grounds have been the venue for a number of dramatic productions and concerts. Here an open-air night-time production of *Camelot* takes place in 1974. (Copyright *Western Mail and Echo*)

The launch of Ostreme in 1973, with the aim of raising money for the creation of a community centre in Mumbles, began a tradition that has continued even beyond the building and opening of the Ostreme Centre. As part of the first Ostreme, Mrs Meriel Mathias, suitably dressed for the occasion, cuts the ribbon to open the Madam Patti Walk.

The Ostreme Theatre players take a bow after their performance of *Speeches and Cream* in 1981. Mrs Meriel Mathias was the producer.

Mumbles Carnival, 1981.

Oystermouth church, *c.* 1910. There has been a church at Oystermouth since before the ninth century. Fragments of Roman pottery and the existence of a tessellated floor show that the church is built on, or very near, the site of a Roman building.

Interior of Oystermouth church, *c.* 1910.

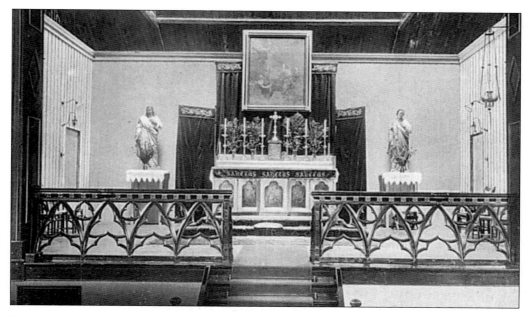

Interior of the church of Our Lady Star of the Sea, *c.* 1950.

Roseland Terrace, Mumbles, *c.* 1905.

Park Avenue, Mumbles, *c.* 1910.

Claremont Villas, Mumbles, *c.* 1905. These were demolished to allow for the building of the parade of shops adjacent to the post office.

Woodville Road, Mumbles, *c*. 1910.

Newton Road, from Newton, with Underhill Park on the right-hand side of the picture, around 1905.

Mumbles cemetery, c. 1920. Created in 1883, the cemetery is, surprisingly, the subject of a number of postcards by various publishers. This one was published by Cornwall Stores of Mumbles.

Oystermouth Church of England School AFC, 1925/26 season.

Oystermouth school football team, 1947/48 season.

Oystermouth school cricket team, champions, 1948. Back row, from left to right: R.E. Bradshaw, L. Harris, D. Griffiths, R. Browning, M. Jones, D.T. Sheehan, G. Thomas. Front row: A. Ockwell, J. Rogers, J. Pressdee, R. Jones, -?-.

Oystermouth school Coronation celebrations, 1953.

Oystermouth school Coronation celebrations, 1953. Getting ready for the fancy dress parade.

Oystermouth school Coronation celebrations, 1953. Some of the stars of the fancy dress competition.

Oystermouth school sports day at Underhill Park, 1970. The boys' wheelbarrow race. (Copyright *South Wales Evening Post*)

The girls' sprint race at an Oystermouth school sports day, probably in 1974, and again held at Underhill Park. The houses of Newton can be seen on the hill behind.

Oystermouth school St David's Day, 1974.

Oystermouth infants' school centenary, 1977. The children celebrate in Victorian costume in the grounds of Oystermouth Castle.

Miss Morgan, the reception teacher at Oystermouth infants' school, in Victorian dress at the school's centenary celebrations in 1977.

Oystermouth infants' school. A class of seven-year-old pupils in 1972.

With the closure of the Oystermouth Junior Comprehensive School, the buildings were earmarked as the new site for Oystermouth County Primary School. However, the site was full of temporary classrooms that were no longer required.

The temporary classrooms severely restricted the playground space.

The school site looked unsightly and cramped.

The old temporary classrooms were in a very poor state of repair.

Work soon began on the demolition of the temporary classrooms.

A JCB managed to get onto the site to make the demolition work easier.

Progress was rapid, with the buildings soon reduced to steel skeletons.

Soon there was only rubble left.

The site was then landscaped and extra playground space created.

Where once rusting buildings stood as eyesores, flower beds brightened the school grounds.

Oystermouth Keep Fit class in the 1950s.

On this 1905 postcard view across Underhill Park to Newton, the publisher has rather poetically used the description 'Langland Vale'.

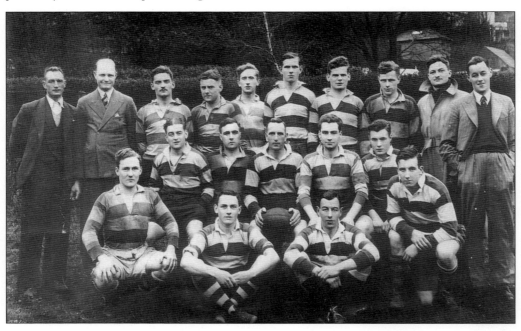

Underhill Park is the home of Mumbles RFC. Here the 1st XV for the 1938/39 season are pictured. Back row, from left to right: F. Cook, N. Hope, N. Woolacott, L. Kettle, W. Lloyd, H. Smaile, L. Lewis, J. Devonall, E. Beynon. Centre row, seated: W. Rees, I. Williams, C. Hopkins (captain), T. McDonald, I. Hixson. Front row: K. Thatcher, O. Smith, G. Beynon, ? Perkins.

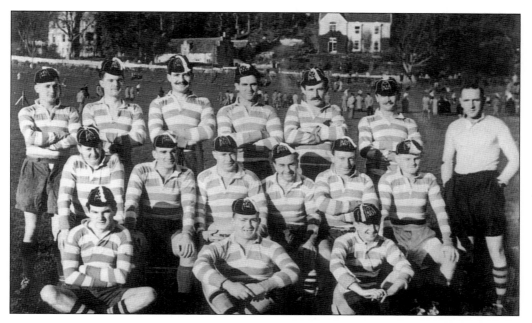

Mumbles RFC Outcasts XV, 1951. Back row, from left to right: O. Williams, I. Lewis, J. Williams, E. Gorman, J. Nener, T. Cox, C. Hopkins. Middle row: P. Pickwick, P. Lebars, I. Hixson (captain), I. Matthews, G.N. Jones, R. Hopkins. Front row: J. Burridge, E. Burns, T. Charles. This team was made up of retired players and exiles and they played the club 1st XV for the George Harbridge Trophy on Boxing Day morning in 1951.

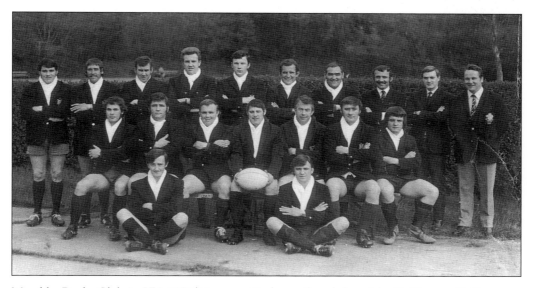

Mumbles Rugby Club 1st XV, 1970/71 season. Back row, from left to right: B. Thomas, R. Bateman, P.Hunt, A. Davies, P. Evans, D. Morgan, D. Jones, C. Williams, J. Anderson, J. Yates. Middle row: R. Davies, D. Baker, D. Price, J. Lamb, M. Evans, D. Robins, G. Beynon. Front row: P. Hixson, P. Bessant.

In the immediate post-war years Mrs Eunice Stockton organized an informal dancing school at her home. Also, she and her husband produced pantomimes and travelled far and wide through south and west Wales performing them. This photograph was taken at the 1949 Christmas party.

A scene from the 1949 pantomime, *Babes in the Wood*. (Copyright *South Wales Evening Post*)

The cast of *Babes in the Wood*, 1949. (Copyright *South Wales Evening Post*)

A scene from the 1950 production of *Cinderella*. (Copyright *South Wales Evening Post*)

Newton Road looking towards the junction with New Well Lane, *c.* 1912. The huge horse chestnut tree was a well-known source of conkers for many years.

Three
Newton to West Cross

Looking up Southward Lane towards the junction with Newton Road, *c.* 1880. Newton at this time was a small rural community quite separate from Oystermouth.

The same view as the last picture, but taken in 1910. The cottage in the centre of that picture has now been replaced by a much larger building housing the post office. Newton post office first opened in 1885, the first sub-postmaster being Charles Williams, described in contemporary directories as a 'grocer and baker, Post Office, maker of Smith's patent Hovis bread, which is a cure for indigestion'.

The previous picture shows the post office with some kind of shuttering, which might indicate that the shop was not open at the time the photograph was taken. This postcard from around 1918 gives a closer view of the post office, and it can be seen that the windows are not in any way obstructed.

A snowy day in Newton, c. 1920. As can be seen, the post office now has a nameboard above the window.

A picture of Southward Lane, complete with delivery cart and carefully posed children, probably dating from around 1890.

Southward Lane looking south, *c.* 1880, with the Rock and Fountain Inn on the right-hand side. The man is seated on the mounting block outside the public house.

The same view, photographed in 1907, shows the mounting block still in situ but very few other changes.

New Well Lane, looking towards
Underhill Park, c. 1880.

New Well Lane, c. 1912. The developments around Underhill Park can be clearly seen.

This photograph of the junction of Newton Road and New Well Lane dates from around 1910 and was taken after a heavy fall of snow.

The Nottage end of Southward Lane, *c.* 1920.

Brynfield Road, Newton, with the church at the far end, in around 1920.

St Peter's church, Newton, c. 1910. Today the pine trees, planted in 1903 when the church was built, are great trees that hide the church building most effectively.

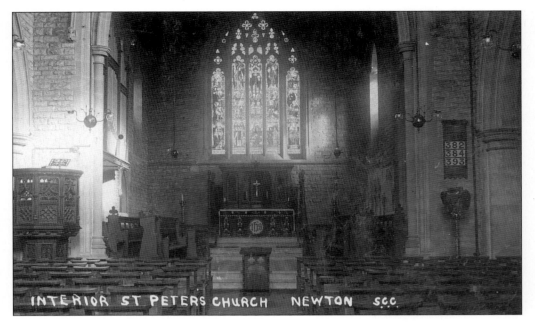

Interior of St Peter's church, Newton, *c.* 1920.

Newton Primary School was opened in 1968. Here some girls prepare for netball practice at the newly-opened school, whilst in the background a group of boys limber up for rugby training.

A class of infants pose for the camera at Newton Primary School in around 1974.

Modelling with clay at Newton Primary School, 1974.

Practising telephone technique at Newton Primary School, 1974.

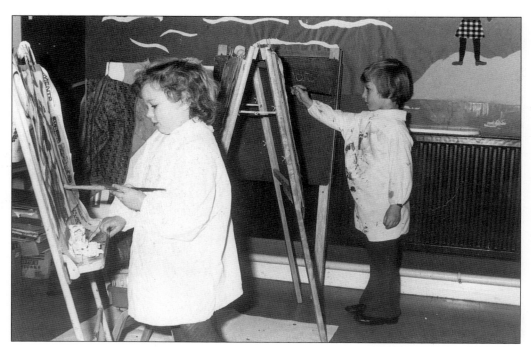

An art lesson in progress at Newton Primary School, 1974.

Young artists prepare their paints, Newton Primary School, 1974.

Getting down to basics at Newton Primary School, 1974.

The cast of Newton Primary School's production of *Joseph and his Amazing Technicolour Dreamcoat*, 1981.

A song from the Newton Primary School production of *Smuggle me a Secret*, 1982.

The cast of Newton Primary School's production of *Smuggle me a Secret* take their bows, 1982.

Infant girls dressed for St David's Day at Newton Primary School, 1978. (Copyright *South Wales Evening Post*)

Junior girls dressed for St David's Day, Newton Primary School, 1978. (Copyright *South Wales Evening Post*)

Celebrating the planting of trees on some open ground at Newton Primary School in around 1985.

Girls' Friendly Society (GFS) stall at a fête at St Peter's church, Newton, in around 1959.

Newton Womens' Institute choir, *c.* 1955.

Newton Womens' Institute folk dancing team, 1950s.

Newton Womens' Institute nativity play, 1956. (Copyright *South Wales Evening Post*)

Some residents of Newton (with guests) set off on a charabanc outing sometime in the 1920s. Charabanc outings were very popular at a time when people did not generally move outside their communities more than once or twice a year.

Alexandra Terrace, Norton, *c.* 1905.

The now defunct Norton Womens' Institute, 1960.

The floor of the quarry at Norton Limeworks, 1923. As well as horse and cart, 30 cwt drams were used to carry the limestone rock to the lime kilns.

Some of the buildings at Norton Limeworks, 1923.

Limekiln Road, Norton, 1923.

Norton Limeworks, 1968.

View of Mumbles from Norton, 1912. This photograph was taken from the limeworks and the top of the lime kilns can be seen in the foreground, along with a steam-driven lorry owned by Bennett Bros.

View across Swansea Bay with Norton in the foreground in around 1930. Lying to the north of Oystermouth, the name 'Norton' derives from 'North town'. A post office was opened in Norton just before the Second World War as a response to the growing residential development in the area.

View over Swansea Bay from West Cross Lane, 1965. Swansea Bay has been compared with the Bay of Naples for its sweeping majesty. On a warm summer evening, with the lights shining around the bay and reflecting in the water, it is easy to be beguiled by such a comparison.

New housing in Alderwood Road, West Cross, 1951. During the 1950s a large municipal housing estate was built at West Cross.

Mr Harry Hoare taking his ease at Alderwood Road, West Cross, 1951. Mr Hoare was an early resident of the new municipal housing at West Cross.

Aeriel view of Grange Primary School, c. 1951. Part of the site later became St David's
Roman Catholic Primary School. The image is not very sharp, but it provides a valuable
document of how the area used to look.

An annual Easter bonnet parade has been a long tradition at Grange Primary School. Here pupils pose on the climbing frame in around 1969.

Easter bonnets 1970s style at Grange Primary School.

More Easter bonnets from the 1970s. The high climbing frame no longer exists, and indeed it would not now be considered safe. The area of playground where this climbing frame stood is now part of the St David's School playground.

A PE lesson at Grange Primary School, 1974. Such equipment and lack of safety mats would surely earn the condemnation of health and safety inspectors today.

Knuckling down to work at Grange Primary School, 1974.

Art at Grange Primary School, 1974. The free school milk seen on the tables was soon to be abolished thanks to the-then Education Secretary, who was jeered by opponents as 'Margaret Thatcher, milk snatcher'.

Watching television at Grange Primary School, 1974.

Science work at Grange Primary School, 1974. Interestingly, a chart on the wall tells which children would be staying at Grange and which would be transferring to the new Whitestones Primary School which opened that year.

St David's Day at Grange Primary School, 1971.

Mumbles Road, West Cross, c. 1910. The area of West Cross was once heavily wooded and legend has it that oak trees were felled here to build ships for Sir Francis Drake's fleet that defeated the Spanish Armada.

Four
The Mumbles Railway

The popularity of the Mumbles Railway meant that there were many postcards published devoted to it. Dating from around 1900, this one shows a steam-hauled train at Oystermouth station.

Steam had been introduced in 1877 and was used in conjunction with horse-power until 1896, when the horse-drawn vehicles were withdrawn. In this picture dating from around 1902, a steam-hauled train of single and double-decker carriages passes the old Roman bridge at Blackpill.

The Mumbles train at the Slip, c. 1910. The message on the back reads, 'this extraordinary-looking train runs alongside the road from Swansea to Mumbles – six miles'.

Line up of cars at the terminus at Mumbles Pier, c. 1905.

Train leaving Mumbles, c. 1902. In the summer months especially, the trains were full to capacity.

King George V and Queen Mary visited Swansea on 19 July 1920 and travelled on the Mumbles Railway, using this special train.

Oystermouth station, 1920.

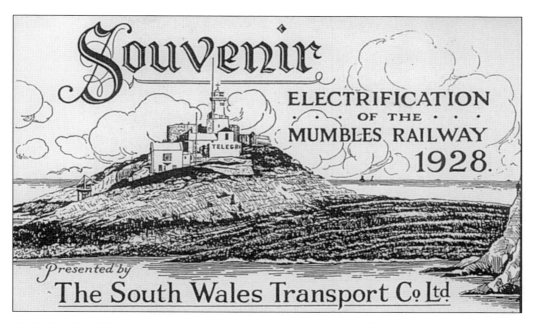

Souvenir

ELECTRIFICATION OF THE MUMBLES RAILWAY 1928.

Presented by
The South Wales Transport Co Ltd

On 1 March 1920 the last steam train ran on the Mumbles Railway, for the line had been electrified, and new electric cars carried the passengers. This souvenir was issued in 1928 to mark the impending change.

OLD AND NEW MUMBLES TRAIN

This postcard, published late in 1929, shows the old steam train and the new electric train. Journey times had been cut from forty-five minutes to nineteen minutes and a much more frequent service offered. The growth in passenger traffic was such that in 1945 almost five million passengers travelled on the railway.

Just out of Rutland Street terminus, a train picks up speed.

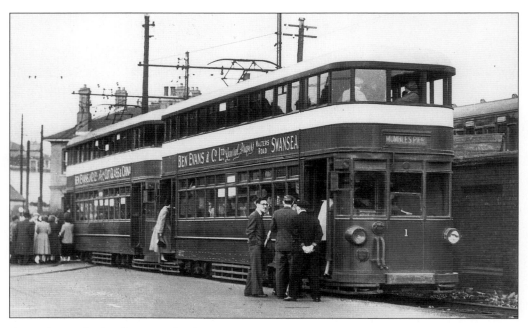

A train is readied to leave Rutland Street for Mumbles Pier.

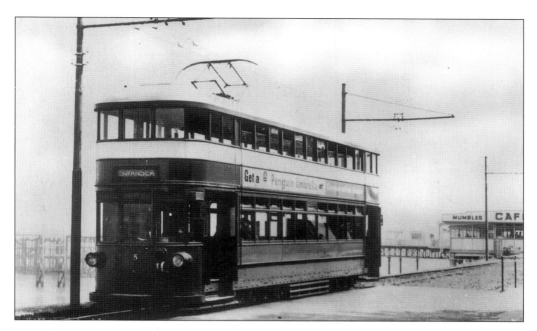

An early morning service waits at the Pier terminus.

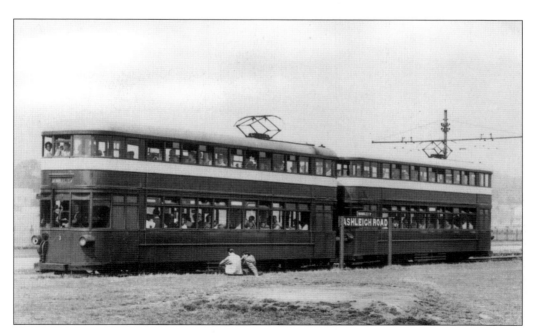

A train stops at Ashleigh Road.

Mumbles Railway 150th Anniversary
Programme of Events

TUESDAY, 29th JUNE, 1954

THE COMPANY HEREBY GIVES NOTICE THAT ON TUESDAY, 29th JUNE, 1954, THE TRAIN SERVICE BETWEEN RUTLAND STREET AND MUMBLES PIER WILL BE SUSPENDED AFTER THE RUNNING OF THE 9.19 a.m. FROM RUTLAND STREET AND 9.42 a.m. FROM THE PIER, AND WILL BE RESUMED AT 12.55 p.m. FROM RUTLAND STREET AND 1.18 p.m. FROM THE PIER. BETWEEN THESE TIMES A FREQUENT 'BUS SERVICE WILL BE SUBSTITUTED.

10.15–10.40 a.m.	Dancing on the green at Southend by children of the Mumbles Schools.
10.45–11. 0 a.m.	Demonstrations of physical training on the railway line at Southend by boys of Oystermouth Secondary School.
11. 0–11.15 a.m.	Commentary.
11.15 a.m.	Official party will arrive at Southend Station.
11.20–11.50 a.m.	Horse-drawn " train " of the early 19th century will travel from Oystermouth station to Southend. This will be followed by a steam train, to commemorate the transition from horse to steam traction in 1877. To complete the procession, there will be an electric train, representing the introduction of electric traction in 1929.
12. 0 noon	Formal opening of the Mumbles Railway Exhibition at the Pier Hotel by Mr. W. T. James, O.B.E., Chairman of the South Wales Transport Co., Ltd.
12.20–8. 0 p.m.	Mumbles Railway Exhibition at the Pier Hotel open to the public.
12.30– 9. 0 p.m.	The carriages used for the horse and steam trains will be available for inspection at Mumbles Pier.
12.15–12.45 p.m.	Marionette Show at the Casino Ballroom, Newton Road, Mumbles. Admission free.
2.15– 2.45 p.m. 3. 0– 3.30 p.m.	do. do.
3.30– 5. 0 p.m.	Band Concert at Mumbles Pier.
6.30 p.m.	Launching of the lifeboat at Mumbles Pier.
6.30 p.m. onwards	Yacht racing.
7. 0– 8.30 p.m.	Band Concert at Mumbles Pier.

The 150th anniversary of the Mumbles Railway was celebrated with a programme of events.

CELEBRATION LUNCHEON

AT THE

GUILDHALL, SWANSEA

IN HONOUR OF THE

150th Anniversary

OF THE

Swansea & Mumbles Railway

One event was a celebration luncheon.

A train passes Southend heading for Mumbles Pier.

A train arrives at the Mumbles Pier terminus.

A single car passes the small boats drawn up on the foreshore at Southend. For part of its route the railway ran just above the high water line.

DEATH
OF THE
MUMBLES RAILWAY
IMPORTANT NOTICE TO OUR CUSTOMERS.

On OCTOBER 12th, 1959, the Mumbles Railway will terminate at Southend Station—where Buses will connect to bring Customers direct to the top of the Pier Hill. The same procedure will operate on the return journey.

This method of transport will operate from Monday, Oct. 12th, until the beginning of January, when the Railway officially closes, and the New Bus Service direct to the present Pier Train Terminus begins.

The Management of this Hotel regrets the inconvenience this arrangement will cause—but trust that you will all bear with us during this period.

Pier Hotel, Mumbles. (Signed) J. W. BARTLETT, Manager.

R. J. COTTLE, PRINTER, NEWTON, MUMBLES.

The proprietor of the Pier Hotel placed this notice in the local press to mourn the passing of the Mumbles Railway, which closed on 5 January 1960.

SOUTH WALES
TRANSPORT CO., LTD.

(Associated with the British Electric Traction Co., Ltd.)

REVISED SERVICES TO BE INTRODUCED
ON THE

ABANDONMENT OF
THE MUMBLES RAILWAY

ON THE DISCONTINUANCE OF THE MUMBLES RAILWAY THE FOLLOWING NEW SERVICES AND IMPROVED FACILITIES WILL BE INTRODUCED :—

NEW SERVICES

Route 77   **MUMBLES PIER—PONTLASSE CROSS**
EVERY 12 MINUTES.

Route 94   **OYSTERMOUTH SQ.—RUTLAND STREET**
EVERY 12 MINUTES DURING PEAK PERIODS.

IMPROVED FACILITIES

WEEKLY AND SEASON TICKETS WILL BE INTRODUCED FOR THE FIRST TIME OVER ALL STAGES ON SERVICES 40, 85, 92 & 93.

With the closure, it was left to the bus service to meet the demand for public transport on the route from Swansea to Mumbles Pier. The South Wales Transport Company published a booklet outlining the new and revised services that were to be introduced.

Five
Mumbles Lifeboat

Mumbles lifeboat *James Stevens No. 12*, which capsized at Port Talbot on 31 January 1903. The first lifeboat came to Swansea in 1835, being stationed at the South Dock. The station was removed to Mumbles in 1863.

The boarding boat (formerly the *Richard*) returning from the Mixon on 24 April 1907. The Mixon Sands were a particularly dangerous area of the Bristol Channel and the frequent loss of ships there was the reason for the founding of a lifeboat at Swansea.

The William Gammon, *c.* 1965. This lifeboat was named after the coxswain of the *Edward Prince of Wales*, which was lost on the 24 April 1947, with her entire crew.